Volume X, Number 11

Significant Issues Series

Organizing for National Security

by Robert E. Hunter

The Center for Strategic
and International Studies
Washington, D.C.

Library of Congress Cataloging-in-Publication Data

Hunter, Robert Edwards, 1940-
   Organizing for national security.

   (Significant issues series, ISSN 0736-7136; v. 10, no. 11)
   1. National Security Council (U.S.)   2. United States—National security.   I. Title.   II. Series.
UA23.H936   1988   353.0089   88-25598
ISBN 0-89206-122-7

The Center for Strategic and International Studies is a research organization founded in 1962 to foster scholarship and public awareness of emerging international issues on a broad, interdisciplinary basis. It is bipartisan and nonprofit. Its areas of research are selected in consultation with its governing bodies, and its work is entirely unclassified.

© 1988
The Center for Strategic and International Studies
Washington, D.C.

All Rights Reserved

Contents

About the Author	iv
Foreword *by Amos A. Jordan*	v
Introduction *by Robert M. Kimmit*	vii
Organizing for National Security	1
The National Security Council	3
Personnel	5
The National Security Adviser	7
Advising the President	16
The System in Practice	18
The Exceptions	19
Foreign, Economic, and Domestic Policy	21
Strategic Direction	25
Conclusions	32
Notes	34
Appendix: Checklist of Top-Priority Recommendations for Presidential Candidates and the President-Elect	41

About the Author

Robert E. Hunter is director of European studies and senior fellow in Middle Eastern studies at the Center for Strategic and International Studies in Washington, D.C. He has been special adviser on Lebanon to the Speaker of the House of Representatives and lead consultant to the National Bipartisan Commission on Central America (the Kissinger Commission).

During the Carter administration, Dr. Hunter served on the National Security Council staff as director of West European affairs (1977-1979) and then as director of Middle East affairs (1979-1981). Prior to that, he was foreign policy adviser to Senator Edward M. Kennedy, senior fellow at the Overseas Development Council, research associate at the International Institute for Strategic Studies, and adviser to Vice President Hubert Humphrey. He served on the White House staff during the Johnson administration and has written speeches for leading Democratic Party figures for more than 20 years.

Dr. Hunter was educated at Wesleyan University (B.A. and Phi Beta Kappa) and the London School of Economics (Ph.D. and Fulbright scholar), where he also taught. He has been professorial lecturer at Georgetown University and the Johns Hopkins University School of Advanced International Studies. He serves on the Wesleyan University Board of Trustees.

Among his many publications are *The Soviet Dilemma in the Middle East* (Institute for Strategic Studies, 1969), *Security in Europe* (Indiana University Press, 1989, third ed.), *Presidential Control of Foreign Policy* CSIS Washington Paper (Praeger, 1982), *NATO: The Next Generation* (Westview, 1985) (editor), and *European Peace Movements* (Transaction, 1985) (coeditor). He writes regularly for the *Los Angeles Times* and the *Army/Navy/Air Force Times* and appears frequently on radio and television.

Foreword

National elections demand the best of the policy research community. National policies are critiqued and reviewed, new positions are formulated by candidates, and the public and their leaders join in a debate about the course of the country. The best policy institutes contribute to this process with sound, fresh ideas on the compelling issues of the day.

This publication is the eighth in a series designed by the Center for Strategic and International Studies (CSIS) to infuse a strategic perspective into the election year debate on the international role of the United States. This project stands apart from similar sounding ones in a number of important ways.

First, believing that effective leadership necessitates a careful choice of initiatives, we seek primarily to set priorities. A long laundry list of policy initiatives by executive departments cannot be an instrument of either leadership or bipartisan action. But a series of concise statements about select problems, opportunities, and action steps can help keep the nation's international course on track.

Second, we seek to identify the boundaries of tomorrow's policy debate instead of simply projecting forward the contents of today's debate. By identifying emerging problems, we enable the policy community to begin grappling with them before they become crises.

Third, this project addresses national leadership as a whole, not just key individuals in a new administration. An analytical framework that focuses on executive branch concerns to the exclusion of congressional and private-sector perspectives is likely to be worn down very quickly.

Finally, this project draws on intellectual contributions from a full range of individuals involved in CSIS study groups, steering committees, and other networks so that the final result reflects not simply the idiosyncratic views of the CSIS staff but rather is a distillation of the best thinking of a broad cross section of the nation's most talented and experienced policy experts.

This volume focuses on procedural or institutional reforms that might enhance the efficacy of the international policies of the United States. Authored by Robert Hunter, director of European studies at CSIS and widely recognized as one of the most thoughtful students of the policy-making process and especially of the National Security Council, the paper sets out specific recommendations for refining the policy process based on the lessons of the last 40 years.

CSIS is grateful to Robert Hunter for his thoughtful analyses and pragmatic recommendations. It is important to note that CSIS as an institution does not adopt positions on policy issues before the nation; rather, the views expressed in this publication series are solely those of the contributing scholars and study groups.

As a research institute focused primarily on the U.S. role in the world, CSIS looks to the next national election and to the 1990s with both anticipation and concern. The challenges will be keen. The opportunities will be plentiful. With this series of publications, we hope to take the informed observer beyond the rhetoric of political debate to see the complexities of our world and to build consensus about policies that are both realistic and farsighted.

Amos A. Jordan
Vice Chairman, Board of Trustees
The Center for Strategic and
International Studies

August 1988

Introduction

In recent years, excellent analyses of the National Security Council (NSC) have been written by, among others, I. M. Destler, Robert Hunter, and Zbigniew Brzezinski. These analyses focused on and compared the ongoing operations of the NSC in various administrations. In the paper that follows, however, my former colleague Robert Hunter adds a new and valuable perspective by examining the structural issues that must be considered prior to the inauguration—even prior to the election—for the new president's national security policy to be conducted successfully.

Robert Hunter knows from whence he speaks. After serving in the White House under President Lyndon Johnson and on the personal staff of Senator Edward Kennedy, Hunter joined the NSC staff in 1977 under President Jimmy Carter. From 1977 until 1979, he was the senior staff member responsible for Europe, and from 1979 until 1981 he had senior staff responsibility for the Middle East.

Hunter's central points should be on the minds of the candidates from their nominating conventions, if not before. National security is a vital, complex responsibility that adheres from the moment of inauguration, and the transition period alone is not sufficient time to prepare for this awesome responsibility. Hunter also emphasizes that the new president's range of choice in organizing national security affairs is, or should be, significantly restricted by reference to precepts garnered from the experiences of recent administrations.

Hunter makes two very strong points early in his monograph. First, the new president should not waste time and energy at the outset of his administration pursuing reorganization initiatives that require legislative action. Second, in assembling a topflight national security team, the new president should seek both harmony and tension, because dynamic and creative tension benefits a president who values strongly argued options. The very best papers that I encountered while executive secretary of the NSC addressed issues on which cabinet officers strongly disagreed; consensus documents often did not merit presidential involvement.

I also agree with Hunter that international economics must be recognized, substantively and procedurally, as an integral component of the national security equation. I disagree, however, that we need in the executive office of the president a structure similar to the former Council on International Economic Policy. Instead, I would favor an Economic Policy Council chaired by the secretary of the treasury, who would be made a statutory member of the NSC.

The bottom line of this thoughtful paper is that although the NSC membership is set by statute, the shaping of the NSC system—including additional invitees, committee structure, and composition of the NSC staff—is left wholly to the new president. If the system does not suit his style or meet his expectations, the president may very well ask himself why he did not take time to read Robert Hunter's fine paper.

Robert M. Kimmitt
Partner, Sidley & Austin
Former Executive Secretary,
National Security Council

Organizing for National Security

On January 20, 1989, a new U.S. president will assume office—only 73 days after he is elected. During that brief period of transition, he must create a government and will, therefore, make some of the most far-reaching decisions of his presidency. This is particularly true of policy relating to international affairs. An unrelenting world begins to test the new U.S. president almost from his first day in office, and mistakes can have consequences far beyond the implications of errors in domestic policy.

There is no doubt that a president's wisdom, temperament, ambitions, vision, and capacity for leadership are vital to the success or failure of the presidency in exercising the stewardship of America's role in the world. In addition, the way in which the president organizes and manages the means for carrying out that stewardship is critical not only to his prospects but to those of the nation as well. In recent administrations, this fact has been underlined for the American people. Perhaps qualities of leadership cannot be learned by a new president: they derive from the sum of the president's character and experience on the road to the White House. Effective management in international affairs, however, is very much subject to what the president learns as the office and duties take shape. This effective management is also critical for him as he attempts to take initiatives and set priorities in international affairs—major goals of virtually any new president. With a workable structure for making and carrying out policy, well established by inauguration day, the president can take command and exercise leadership; without it, he risks being handicapped and losing the precious momentum of his first few months in office.

This year, for the first time in 20 years, there is no incumbent U.S. president running for reelection. Thus, there is certain to be a distinct transition from the Reagan administration to the administration of the new president. Presumably, this transition will be less wrenching if George Bush is elected than if Michael Dukakis wins the election. In a Republican administration, there is certain to be some holdover of personnel from one administration to the next, who come with the attendant experience of managing the government. Yet even in this case, the new president will no doubt want to put his own stamp on the office. His temperament and his management style are likely to be different from the incumbent's. In short, whether Bush or Dukakis becomes president, the new president will no doubt want to make some changes in the means of making and carrying out policy affecting the United States' role in the world.

The central theme of this discussion is that the new president will be more restricted in organizing the executive branch for international affairs than would seem to be the case to an outsider. Surely, a president has great latitude in setting up, organizing, staffing, and managing the apparatus of government? Although the U.S. Constitution and various acts of Congress provide constraints, within these constraints the president should have broad discretion.

This may be true in theory. In practice, however, a president will find that he must follow a number of key procedures if he wishes to be able to govern effectively in international affairs. Every president has an individual style of governing that will inevitably play a key part in determining how he conducts the office. Nevertheless, should he violate in any significant way the precepts that follow, he is likely to decrease his chances of being an effective chief executive. This judgment is not based on some abstract notion of the demands of the office, but on an assessment of the strengths and weaknesses of experiments in governance carried out by recent presidents. The lessons that follow are derived from experience, and they are likely to have validity for the next president, whether it is George Bush or Michael Dukakis.

Observers with experience in the National Security Council (NSC) system[1] will recognize that most of the recommendations here relate closely to the way the system evolved during the administrations of Presidents Richard Nixon, Gerald Ford, and Jimmy Carter.[2] The Reagan administration undertook some major departures from the Nixon, Ford, and Carter systems. In recent years, however, the NSC system under the Reagan administration has, in practice, increasingly come to resemble its immediate predecessors. In the following discussion, where practices that have been followed before are recommended, the reasons for doing so are also provided. There are also many recommendations relating to the newer challenges, complexities, and difficulties that the next president of the United States will face in the area of national security policy. Not everything is covered here, but what follows are those issues of process and recommendations for their resolution that are most critical to the president's role and his capacity to govern in international affairs during at least the first part of his term of office.

The National Security Council

To be effective in managing the nation's international affairs—"national security policy" in its broadest sense—a new president must first attend to both process and personnel. The latter is the lifeblood of politics and governance at all levels. Process is often neglected, however, especially by incoming presidents who have not had to lead large bureaucracies. No presidential candidate—who has not already been president—has led a process as complex, demanding, and subtle as making and implementing U.S. national security policy.

By law, key decisions are made in the name of the National Security Act of 1947 by the NSC. This statutory body is relatively modest. It consists of the president, the vice president, the secretaries of state and defense, and three statutory advisers: the chairman of the joint chiefs of staff, the director of central intelligence (DCI) (who, thus far, has also been director of the Central Intelligence Agency), and the director of the Arms Control and Disarmament Agency (ACDA).[3] The next president would be well advised to expand this membership, by invitation or statute, to include other key officials, certainly the assistant to the president for national security affairs (the national security adviser) and the treasury secretary, whose duties are deeply engaged in international affairs. The president should also include the director of the Office of Management and Budget (OMB) and the White House chief of staff in the NSC meetings. Depending on the subject to be considered and the president's personal style of governing, he should also invite one or more of the following officials to take part: the chief White House domestic affairs adviser, the head of the congressional liaison staff, the chairman of the Council of Economic Advisers, key political advisers, and, at times, even his press secretary.

Critics often argue that an extension of informal NSC membership weakens the authority of the body. It is quite the opposite; the NSC should consider the feasibility of foreign affairs policies as well as their theoretical merits. Thus, congressional relations, domestic economics and budget, domestic policy, politics, and press relations are all essential to effective policy. For purposes of frank discussion, however, particular officials should not take part in sensitive meetings.[4]

Yet given the pace of events and the range of decisions that must be made and carried out in the execution of U.S. national security policy, all recent presidents have found the NSC to be a cumbersome device. Indeed, Dwight Eisenhower was the only president who consistently made use of the council as a major tool of managing foreign policy. Ronald Reagan has also made significant use of this formal body.

Recent administrations have thus developed an interlocking group of committees and sets of formal papers that permit an orderly review of issues and, when warranted, preparation for presidential decision. Having such a system is critical; a complex organism like the U.S. government, acting on national security policy, must have a high degree of order and predictability if it is to function effectively. Different parts of the government must understand what is expected of them and have a sense of how they should respond to presidential direction. This can only be effective when process becomes routine. If it does not, the NSC system can never hope to deal with the mass of challenges and make the required decisions.

The recommendations that appear below are modest in a particular sense: they are sparing on the subject of governmental reorganization. In general, a president is well served if he can, at least at the outset, avoid having to change the formal structures of government, especially when these structures are embodied in law. Thus, there may be merit in reducing the number of assistant secretaries of state, for example, but many of these offices are provided for in law, and a president could lose valuable time, energy, and political capital with Congress by trying to make changes. Each new president must decide for himself the exceptions to this guideline, but it is useful at the beginning of an administration for a president to avoid changing formal structures until, by experience, he can judge what institutional changes will best suit his needs and those of the nation.

Personnel

To develop an administration that will effectively aid the president in discharging his duties in international affairs, he must pay particular attention to the individuals he selects for key posts. Because of their critical importance to the nation, these can be among the most important decisions of his presidency. In addition, if a president later finds that he must replace cabinet-level officials in international affairs, he is likely to pay a higher price than he would in the domestic arena, in terms of his administration's credibility both at home and abroad.

In appointing people to senior international affairs posts, most incoming presidents are at a disadvantage. U.S. presidential elections rarely turn on foreign policy issues and certainly not on a candidate's comprehensive knowledge of them. Nor is there a natural tendency for a candidate to meet a wide variety of individuals in the field. This situation is quite different from domestic and economic affairs, which are the bread-and-butter issues of elections. In the normal course of events, a candidate will meet a wide variety of individuals who could be considered for senior office. Furthermore, in domestic affairs, satisfying different constituencies and interest groups is a major part of staffing an administration. In international affairs, by contrast, these factors are far less consequential. Here, qualities of knowledge about the outside world and sound judgment must outweigh other criteria.

Many incoming presidents have been adept at choosing their key aides in foreign and defense policy, even many of the deputies. But this skill comes from conscious effort, generally begun well before the heat and distractions of the election campaign. A newly elected president who has not met a wide variety of talented people in international affairs is likely to become a prisoner of the opinions of others in making his selections and risks losing a major measure of latitude and control from the beginning of his presidency.

It would be pointless in this study to make recommendations about the particular people whom a new president should choose to staff his administration. But some criteria can be suggested, bearing in mind the uniqueness of each president, his style of governing, his background and relative experience in international affairs, and his capacity for judgment and leadership. In short, the president must be responsible for choosing those people whom he believes will best serve him and the interests of the nation. No one can prescribe this for him.

In general, however, any president will benefit from the realization that the time is long since past when major aspects of U.S. national security policy could be entrusted to individuals with general talent and experience in public policy, yet lacking particular knowledge of, or vocation for, international affairs. This does not mean that the responsibility for policy-making should be relegated to regional or functional experts who have no broader experience or understanding. Rather, a president and his senior advisers must be able to evaluate expert views and exercise informed judgment about the worth of competing ideas.

Of course, knowledge of foreign, defense, and economic issues—among others—does not exhaust the requirements for an effective national security team. A president must have knowledgeable political advisers in these and other areas, individuals who can relate effectively to Congress and who understand the public's mood and attitudes, as well as advisers whose skills go beyond the narrow definition of international affairs. There would certainly be value in selecting some senior officials from Congress—members who have extensive experience in foreign, defense, or economic policy. This is especially important at a time when distinctions between foreign and domestic policy have become blurred.

The key point is that there can be no room for the amateur or the second-rate: the United States' changing position in the world will not tolerate it. An incoming president must also avoid one other potential difficulty: being dominated in his selections by the competition to fill national security positions. In many domestic areas, the ratification by interest groups of contenders for office often reflects the disposition of issues and the politics necessary for a president to be effective. This is not necessarily true in foreign and defense policy. A new president needs the best people he can find with requisite skills to serve him and the nation. All the individuals whom he would ideally like to have, however, may not emerge from the competition within the U.S. international affairs community.

A president would be well served to know his own strengths and weaknesses, his own mind about the importance he wishes to give to international issues, and the rough order of priorities he intends to set among the broad range of alternatives. This self-knowledge can be important in guiding his choice of top administration officials. In the process, he must also be attentive to a skill that does not necessarily come naturally to senior officials: the ability to manage. This quality need not repose in cabinet officials; however, if it does not, these officials must be enjoined to ensure that senior deputies have this vital capability.

A president must also ensure that he has one or more top-level advisers able to think conceptually about national security policy, to relate disparate issues to one another and to the whole, and to devise policies that can express a strategic direction for the nation. Some presidents themselves have this capacity. Those who do not, however, must ensure that they have it close at hand. The days when national security policy could just be the sum of individual policies are over, and a president must recognize this when making appointments.[5]

This point is closely related to another key issue: the balance of temperaments and viewpoints among the president's key international affairs advisers. There is merit in seeking a high degree of harmony and compatibility in ideas, attitudes, and working style with the chief executive. This objective must not be pressed to the extreme, however, or the president will risk limiting the range of advice available to him. He should strike a balance. The president should have people who are able to work together and with him to conduct the nation's international business, yet ensure that he does not become a prisoner of his advisers, of particular attitudes, or of the overall NSC system. In this regard, it is useful for the president to remember that when all of his advisers agree, all could be wrong. Dynamic tension among advisers can be of great benefit to a president. Ultimately, the choices are his, and he will be held accountable for them.[6]

The National Security Adviser

To take charge of national security policy and to shape it according to his views, a new president must first attend to his own household within the NSC. By custom, the president's key international affairs assistant within the White House is the national security adviser. Given the pivotal role that this individual can play, plus the inescapable responsibility of the president to define the NSC adviser's role, this position is singled out here for particular treatment.[7]

In recent years, the role of the NSC adviser has often been controversial. This is natural for a variety of reasons. Most important, the NSC adviser has been the focus of a major shift of bureaucratic power and authority from the periphery to the center. Key cabinet heads in national security have progressively lost authority, which has been gathered in the White House and, to a large degree, has been invested in the NSC adviser. Indeed, this position was created in fact rather than in law, and its role grew steadily through the 1960s and 1970s. Only in the early 1980s was there a significant effort to downgrade the importance of this position, and that effort clearly failed. If the NSC adviser is to be effective within the government, even if he or she is not a significant policy adviser, there must be unimpeded access to the president. At the very least, the management of crises and coordinated briefings require this step.

In attempting to prescribe the proper role for the national security adviser in making and carrying out policy, it is useful to separate those functions the adviser must perform from those that are at the president's discretion. It is confusion on this point that has produced most of the valid questioning about the role of the office.

In the modern NSC system, the NSC adviser and the staff—collectively referred to as the "NSC" or the "NSC staff"—have had primary responsibility for seeing that the president is well served in the execution of four key functions:
- ensuring that the president receives the information he needs to be able to act as chief executive in international affairs;
- conveying presidential initiatives or requests for information, ideas, advice, and recommendations to other parts of the U.S. government;
- providing general oversight of the implementation of policy; and,
- coordinating the making of policy.[8]

The first three of these functions have led to little dispute within the government, provided that NSC advisers and their staffs have followed a key rule for effectiveness: playing fair with the rest of the government. Proximity to the president carries with it inherent powers. If those powers are abused, an administration will rapidly lose the mutual trust that is indispensable for it to operate effectively. Both the president and the nation will suffer.

Information

Provided that the NSC staff does not censor or otherwise impede the flow of information to the president from key cabinet officials and other advisers, it is credited with responsibility for providing the president what he needs to know, when it is needed, as well as ensuring that he is not overwhelmed with so much detail that he will be unable to make sense of the whole. This job requires considerable judgment, but it is one that the NSC, aided by the staff of the Situation Room—the information-processing center in the basement of the White House West Wing—has traditionally provided without much opposition from other parts of the government. Through this role, the distinction is drawn between information that can form the basis for making decisions and the particular ideas of individual presidential advisers and departments. In the latter regard, the NSC staff must be sensitive not to impose its own view on what is transmitted to the president—including regular, even daily, reports from cabinet officials, such as the secretaries of state and defense. These other senior advisers must be assured of having direct and personal access to him.

At the same time, the NSC staff can assist the president in achieving one of his most important goals: not becoming the prisoner of any single source of information. It is cliché to say that no one has a monopoly of wisdom. It is equally true that no one source of information is likely to be infallible, nor is any particular intelligence agency likely to be right all the time. A president must constantly be concerned about receiving varied opinions and competitive intelligence—that is, he needs a deliberately structured method of gaining different viewpoints from different parts of the Intelligence Community, from elsewhere in the government, as well as from outside the government. Anyone who becomes president will have acquired this particular skill in areas familiar to him and relevant to gaining political power. In the realm of national security policy, however, many sources of information are not to be found in the public domain. Therefore, a president must develop methods of ensuring a variety of perspectives and a capacity to judge the worth of information presented to him. To these ends, he must also direct the departments and agencies to provide a full range of information to the NSC staff, rather than, for instance, limiting White House access to cable traffic with U.S. missions abroad.

Initiatives

It is important for any new president to give an individual character to the office and to try to shape the course of U.S. national security policy according to his own view of U.S. interests and his own interpretation of his election mandate. Imposing a presidential sense of direction on the activities of the executive branch does not just happen. Left to itself, the bureaucracy will generally continue to propose and implement policies along lines established by the new incumbent's predecessor. This does not mean mindless inertia. Continuity and predictability of policy, unless circumstances change, are more often than not a virtue in the conduct of U.S. national security policy. This does mean, however, that the bureaucracy will not respond to a president's wishes unless it first clearly understands what he wants. At the very least, this is a simple matter of communication and, for initiatives that go beyond what a president has publicly proposed, it requires communication on a confidential basis through government channels.

To a degree, the role of communicator can be played by heads of departments and agencies, on the basis of presidential directions given at meetings of the cabinet, NSC, or smaller gatherings. In recent administrations, however, the NSC adviser and staff have played a key part in providing this channel of communication, especially in establishing routine procedures—one of the key objectives of effective management in international affairs. As presidents discover, there is merit in having a regularized method of conveying their wishes, of creating a record, and of minimizing the risks of miscommunication. There needs to be an orderly means of ensuring that all parties to a president's decision understand clearly what he wants. Like the proverbial automobile accident, different observers of presidential decisions tell different stories, and someone must keep tabs on what is actually to be done.[9] When the president himself is the source of an administration's initiatives—rather than, for example, the secretary of state—the NSC staff should continue to provide this functional service for the rest of the government, and it should be the repository of presidential directives.

In some recent administrations—for example, those of Presidents Nixon and Carter—the NSC adviser and staff have also played a key role in causing reconsideration of a wide range of existing policies, especially at the outset, as a means of helping to create new patterns of thinking and bureaucratic interaction even when new policy initiatives have not resulted. This stirring of the pot can be a valuable device to elicit new views. It is not strictly a question of initiative, however, to the extent it is deriving ideas from the rest of the government rather than merely communicating presidential desires and perspectives.

This process of communicating initiatives or requests for them can benefit from having a formal structure. In recent administrations, this has generally taken the form of memoranda sent from the White House to relevant executive branch departments and agencies. Depending on importance and subject matter, these memoranda have been signed either by the president or by the NSC adviser and routed through the NSC system. Many are negotiated in advance with other parts of the government. Indeed, such a memorandum can originate with the secretary of state but become "official" by coming from the president's office or the NSC. What these memoranda are called is less important than the role they play in stimulating new thought, producing policy recommendations, and introducing order and routine into most government actions in international affairs.[10]

Responses to these memoranda by various parts of the government can then provide a basis for formal consideration of policy. This particular method is not critical; some method of regularizing the consideration of policies is necessary, however. Otherwise, an ad hoc approach to policy development can quickly lead to chaos, paralysis, or some other form of bureaucratic and institutional malfunction.

Oversight of Implementation

For any president, perhaps the most difficult—and certainly the most frustrating—aspect of governing within the executive branch is ensuring that decisions are carried out. Bureaucracies tend to be conservative; thus, they often attempt to resist any major deflection from existing policy. There needs to be a method of monitoring performance and following through on a president's wishes. At the same time, however, presidential decisions may exceed policy tolerance or the nation's capabilities, so there needs to be a means for review and reconsideration. As the only part of the National Security Council system that responds exclusively to the president—as opposed to a continuing bureaucracy with its institutional interests and career professionals—the NSC staff is well situated to provide oversight of policy implementation, especially to ensure that different parts of the government are carrying out their assigned roles.

Oversight must be distinguished from implementation, however. In general, there is wisdom in keeping the NSC adviser and the NSC staff apart from policy implementation. Rarely do they have the expertise, the time, or the personnel to make this possible. Major NSC involvement in implementing policy risks a crossing of wires and detracts from functions unique to the NSC. Most important, there is risk of creating ill will within the rest of the bureaucracy and of eroding the trust that is vital for the NSC staff to do its job. This is especially true regarding issues that are hotly contested within the government. At times, an NSC adviser will have a role to play in diplomacy: for the leadership of some nations, on some issues representation must come from the White House to have the imprimatur of the president. In cases in which this is done, however, it must be closely coordinated with the secretary of state—who, for good order and policy effectiveness, must be the nation's chief diplomat after the president.

Coordination

These three functions—information, initiative, and implementation—can be carried out by the NSC staff in a straightforward manner without creating deep animosities within the rest of the government. A fourth function, however, is both more important and more controversial: coordinating the means of making national security policy. This innocuous-sounding word, "coordinating," contains the essence of the process; thus, it must command the greatest attention in the president's consideration as he organizes his administration in foreign and defense policy.

It is not obvious to the layman that the coordination of policy should be assigned to the NSC adviser and the NSC staff. To outsiders, the secretary of state traditionally appears to be the official most senior, best situated, and presumably most adept at guiding the nation's footsteps abroad. The secretary of defense is invested with most authority in those areas of national security that involve the armed services and the potential use of military power. Economic affairs engage the secretary of the treasury, although there are other contenders.

Indeed, more than one recent president has attempted to decentralize international affairs policy-making—national security policy in its broadest sense. In shorthand, this is cabinet government: to select able cabinet officials, invest them with attendant authority, and expect them to provide effective direction for the nation in their principal areas of competence. Yet in each recent administration in which cabinet government has been tried, it has failed. It has failed not because of inadequacies on the part of cabinet officials or a dearth of wisdom in policies they have advocated. It has failed in large part because no single department or agency of government can exercise sole authority for any major aspect of international affairs for long without cutting across the competence or lines of authority of one or more other parts of the government. No single department or agency can take charge of making bargains on issues and interests that are crucial to governance.

By now, this lesson should be obvious. But it must be continually relearned, as the nation adapts to interdependence—a phenomenon that has become a cliché in political rhetoric but that is often resisted in practice.

Because the United States is no longer able to pursue policies based on a broad and almost instinctive consensus, as was largely true during the Cold War, it is not possible to place primary authority for the coordination of national security policy within the embrace of any single cabinet department or agency. To attempt to do so is to exceed, rapidly and visibly, the competence of that particular department and, at least as important, to incite bureaucratic rivalries that can hardly be contained. Only a fraction of foreign policy can be limited to the purview of the Department of State, even though that department is first among equals in knowledge and ability to advise and act. The Defense Department cannot be custodian of all defense issues, especially when these involve relations with other countries, arms control issues, and budgetary choices. The same is true in area after area. There is no one part of the bureaucracy that can oversee the whole process of making U.S. policy relevant to the broad tasks the nation faces in the outside world.

Increasingly, therefore, the coordination of different strands of interests, alternatives, ideas, recommendations, and policies can only occur in the one place in the executive branch in which there is overarching competence: the office of the president or, by delegation, the office of the NSC adviser and the NSC staff.[11]

Experience in recent administrations indicates that a president has considerable latitude in assigning various management and policy functions in international affairs to different members of his administration. The one function that must be located within the White House is the coordination of policy. This point is neither trivial nor obvious. Indeed, coordination lies at the heart of all policy management and nowhere more than in international affairs—an area that demands that all parts of an administration be able to work together if it is to be effective.

There are also some simple management reasons for locating the coordination function within the White House and, more particularly, within the NSC staff. Bureaucratically, the White House is neutral territory. By attending meetings there, no department or agency official concedes that a rival has primacy on an issue, as might be true if meetings were held at one another's home base. The NSC adviser does not have a large, continuing bureaucracy to which he owes an institutional loyalty, a bureaucracy whose views, almost inevitably, individual cabinet members in each administration increasingly and naturally represent as time passes. The NSC staff works only for the adviser and for the president. The NSC is in a better position than any department or agency beyond the White House (although not necessarily superseding individual officials with close presidential ties) to grasp the implications of ideas and recommendations for a president's interests and overall sense of direction. Also it is uniquely placed at the center of the flow of information to make critical judgments about process.

Furthermore, governance is, in large part, about reconciling competing interests. This is as true of the management of international affairs as it is of domestic affairs, although there is a difference: in international affairs, bureaucratic competition does not represent struggle between the different parts of the U.S. society and economy to the same extent. Nevertheless, in foreign as well as in domestic affairs, essential bargains can only be reached by the individual entrusted with this duty by the American people, the person who has an encompassing purview and political legitimacy—the U.S. president. As national security policy increasingly cuts across bureaucratic lines, there is a corresponding increase in the coordinating role of the NSC adviser, assisted by the NSC staff.

At its best, the NSC adviser and staff act as the traffic cops who monitor the methods of making and carrying out national security policy. They facilitate the process from the beginning by playing a major role in deciding the level at which a decision should be taken. The best rule of thumb is that decisions should be taken at the lowest possible level. Indeed, an effective NSC system should reflect the obverse of the famous slogan "the buck stops here." If a decision is not of sufficient importance—or controversy—to require the involvement of the U.S. president, it should not reach his desk.

The NSC staff is also well placed to help in deciding who, institutionally, should be involved in advising or making decisions. More to the point, the NSC staff must serve the president by ensuring that all officials with legitimate interests in a given issue have a chance to be involved and to be heard. This includes a variety of individuals, not only officials with formal duties in international affairs. The NSC adviser should also ensure that domestic, economic, public affairs, and congressional advisers to the president are also engaged.[12] The NSC staff must perform these important duties to engender trust within the government about the way in which the process is conducted if it is to be effective in serving the president and the country. Fairness is not just a virtue, it is a necessity if the National Security Council system is not to collapse from its internal stresses.

Advising the President

Within the broad framework of this injunction about the role of the NSC in coordinating the means of making policy, a president has a considerable degree of discretion. His interests, temperament, and style of governing become critical.

Most important, he must establish a means of gaining advice from his principal national security officials that will best serve him and enable him to be in charge. In recent administrations, a key judgment has concerned the place the most important presidential adviser will occupy—unless the president wishes to have several who are more or less equal. Controversy involving the role of the NSC adviser most often relates to this point: whether he will be a key policy adviser to the president (perhaps *the* key policy adviser) as well as performing those functions that must be entrusted to someone physically and institutionally in the White House.

If the president wants his key adviser—one who develops a strategic vision—in the person of the NSC adviser, that official must then be doubly scrupulous about engendering trust on the part of other key officials and parts of the government. This is true even if a president wants, in the common phrase, to be "his own secretary of state." In fact, no president and no NSC adviser, however competent, can afford to dispense with a highly structured and well ordered mechanism for making and carrying out national security policy. The president, perhaps working with the NSC adviser or the secretary of state, can play the key role in providing direction for U.S. policy, but unless the overall system works and has the confidence of cabinet officers and the bureaucracy, an administration is destined for major difficulty.

The NSC adviser must also be careful to tailor his role in dealing with the press, the Congress, and foreign leaders, lest he sow confusion about the administration's policies and promote jealousies among his senior colleagues in the NSC system. At times, these roles may gravitate to him because of special competence. For good order and bureaucratic effectiveness, the president should ensure that cabinet officials—especially at the Departments of State, Defense, and Treasury—are adept at the necessary skills. Yet it is unnatural to expect the NSC adviser to abstain totally from these quasi-public functions. Regarding relations with

Congress and some foreign governments, neither the process nor the president would be well served by totally secluding the key White House international affairs staff person. The answer lies in good personal relations between the NSC adviser and his cabinet-level colleagues, plus a routine practice of coordinating statements that represent administrative and presidential viewpoints. The president should make clear from the outset, however, that the secretary of state is his principal spokesperson on foreign affairs.

The structure and composition of the NSC staff are also important matters to be resolved at the outset of an administration. As argued above, the NSC or some White House equivalent must play a key role in policy coordination and communication within the government. The NSC staff can also play a broader role, as extra "eyes and ears" for a president in the bureaucracy, as a separate source of analysis, and as a set of so-called second-guessers.

The last function, however, can cause major difficulty within the government because of the temptation for the NSC staff to dominate policy discussion as a result of inherent institutional advantages that include proximity to the president, lack of a complex bureaucracy, and responsibility for managing the NSC's meetings. There is also risk that a vigorous NSC staff will stimulate jealousy and resentment elsewhere in the government.

Even a president who places key responsibility for policy development in a cabinet department—most likely the State Department—will benefit from having a review by the NSC adviser and staff. This would ensure that the decision-making process has been conducted fairly—that is, in a manner that allows key administration officials to have their say, without which the chances of error would escalate. This review process also has value in that it provides the president with a further check or an added perspective on policy ideas, options, and recommendations. It is for the same reason that a president is well advised to enlist the counsel of domestic, congressional, political, and press relations advisers in making major national security decisions.

The president and his NSC adviser can limit the inherent risks in the role of the NSC staff by keeping it relatively small, by enjoining it to exercise fair play, by ensuring that key cabinet officials have regular access to the president, and by selecting up to half of the NSC staff personnel from the career services. Included in these personnel should be members from the Foreign Service (including information officers with the U.S. Information Agency), the Intelligence Community, the uniformed services, and civil servants from the Departments of State, Defense, Treasury, and others.[13] In the past, such individuals have rarely simply imported attitudes of their home bureaucracies to their service in the White House. Instead, they have helped to ease the flow of information, to provide insight into policy feasibility, to reduce natural jealousies, and generally to link the president's office to the other departments and agencies involved in the NSC system.

The System in Practice

As noted earlier, the functioning of the NSC system depends upon the creation of a committee structure that is allied to the production of standard forms of decision documents and that can be the basic means of national security decision making. There must be exceptions, but in the main, for the institution to work effectively, there must be a set of regularized procedures for managing the complex matters that come before the U.S. government in international affairs.

In a system that must be coordinated from the White House, it is natural that key NSC committees should also have a White House focus. Alternatives have been tried—such as the convening of Senior Interdepartmental Groups (SIGs) in different departments and agencies—but this method has a poor record.[14] These committees should be structured according to the following rules, based on experience:

- they should meet in the White House, which usually means the small basement conference room adjacent to the Situation Room;
- they should be considered a regular means for reaching executive decisions, when it is not necessary to involve the president;
- they should prepare information on those issues that will later be referred for presidential decision; and
- the most senior-level of the committees should hold regular meetings of the president's key advisers without the president in attendance.

This last point is sometimes overlooked. The nature of the discussion and perhaps even the final decision changes when the president is in the room. If the president wishes to use his time wisely and to ensure that advice he receives has been thoroughly reviewed, he should generally insist on this point. Rarely will the president fall victim to the opposing risk—that his key advisers will reach agreement without him and fail to refer a decision to him that he would prefer to make.

In recent administrations, there has been some division over chairmanships in the committee structure between the NSC adviser and cabinet heads, principally the secretary of state. For reasons of bureaucratic neutrality, there is value in entrusting the chairmanship to the NSC adviser, at least on all issues that do not naturally fall within the compass of a particular cabinet official.[15] As with judgments about the level at which National Security Council decisions should be taken, there also need to be decisions about whether meetings are needed and, if so, at what level. Again, within a framework of agreed and understood policy directions, the lower the level at which decisions are taken, the better. In addition to freeing up the time and attention of senior officials, this practice promotes morale and a sense of responsibility within the bureaucracy by emphasizing its role in making decisions as well as implementing them.

By the same token, when there is a major departure in policy, it is important to have a hierarchy of interagency groups, papers, and meetings. This approach is valuable for gaining the best advice, for determining the feasibility of policy, for understanding possible conflicts with other policies, and, often most important, for providing widespread bureaucratic involvement for an emerging policy that has some chance of being successfully implemented, once decided.

The Exceptions

The method of decision making described here may seem cumbersome, even unwieldy. Yet the system provides a sense of routine, predictability, and order. Officials and bureaucrats in different departments and agencies will become accustomed to what is expected of them and of others with whom they work within the NSC system. Indeed, patterns of behavior will develop gradually during the life of an administration, especially as newly appointed officials learn to work effectively with each other and with career officers.

A key virtue of this formal system is that, if properly organized, understood, and operated, it can be accelerated, specially tailored, or even circumvented when circumstances demand. Most often, these circumstances occur when there is a crisis. Obviously, the methods described here cannot serve effectively at all times, especially when events require rapid decision. Unless there is a well-functioning NSC system, however, major crises will paralyze the government in its efforts to deal with anything else. In short, it must be possible to accelerate or short-circuit regular procedures without, in effect, blowing a fuse throughout the government.

Crisis management is one of the areas of national security governance that is most difficult to organize; it is also difficult to recommend hard-and-fast rules for crisis management. Each president will want to develop his own means of bringing to bear what may be his most essential skills in national security: his ability to make sound judgments and decisions under extreme pressures, both foreign and domestic. Whatever formal and informal techniques a president chooses, he will benefit from having created and used a basic NSC system that can deal effectively with non-crisis situations and that can also continue to function "in the background" during the course of a crisis. Increasingly, the United States will be challenged to manage a multitude of different matters simultaneously. In addition, the development of the media intensifies instantaneous public scrutiny and increases the number of areas—such as terrorism and drugs—in which the domestic aspects of issues are at least as important as the international dimensions.

In recent administrations, presidents have adopted a variety of formal techniques for handling crises—and each department and agency has done so, as well.[16] Some presidents utilize formal NSC or cabinet meetings—although, in practice, these often serve the primary function of sustaining public confidence. Some use special action groups or, as in the case of the Cuban missile crisis, a configuration of senior officials not usually brought together. Some have relied on the regular NSC committee system, with meetings in the White House. The Reagan administration, through National Security Decision Directive (NSDD) 2, has vested major responsibility for coordinating crisis management in the vice president.[17] Each method has merit. The key point is that a president, at the outset of his term, should establish procedures that are most likely to serve him well and then should review and amend them as experience dictates. Crises ultimately entail the most personal level of presidential involvement; thus they must be shaped according to his temperament, skills, attitudes, and experience. As a general rule, some derivative of the regular NSC system—the committee structure—would be useful as a first approach, until the president and his team acquire sufficient experience to make seasoned judgments about the method of conducting policy during a crisis.

In recent administrations, other mechanisms outside the regular NSC system have also proved effective. Thus, it has been valuable for the president's top advisers—such as the secretaries of state and defense and the NSC adviser—to meet informally one or more times a week. These sessions can help them to chart overall policy direction, clear up misunderstandings that are better handled away from official meetings, resolve particularly knotty disagreements, devise tactics for public or congressional presentation, and decide on the best means of dealing procedurally with particularly complex or contentious matters. Similar meetings involving the president can also help expedite policy. These encounters with the president often prove most useful if they are preceded by the sessions of the key officials. In both cases, these informal procedures can work for what are, in effect, extraordinary situations, because there also exist workable arrangements that function for ordinary situations. The examples cited here are useful for any administration to follow. The particular methods used or others that should be developed will depend on the unique circumstances of each administration and the relations among top officials and between them and the president.

Foreign, Economic, and Domestic Policy

The definition used here of "national security policy" has been broader than that used in common parlance; it includes a wide variety of U.S. engagements with the outside world. Yet for the United States to achieve virtually any set of useful objectives in its dealings with other countries, the definition must be broadened still further. Indeed, a quick look at the issues now facing the

United States will show that the classic distinction between foreign and domestic issues hardly exists. There is not only the long-standing involvement of war-and-peace issues in domestic politics (as well as in international affairs), but also the budgetary questions about sustaining activities abroad, thereby subtracting from moneys available to be spent at home. In today's world—and increasingly in tomorrow's—a raft of issues will be needed to be viewed from both perspectives. The United States is now more fully engaged in global trade, as a percentage of national income, than ever before. Put simply, U.S. jobs and international affairs are bound together. Two vital areas—food and fuel—are fully mixed in the foreign and domestic arenas. The value of the dollar is no longer set in the United States. In addition, two other issues—terrorism and drugs—are set in both a domestic and a foreign context.

The overlapping of domestic and foreign policy issues is becoming obvious. As a result, it is useful to examine the implications for the organization and management of national security policy in its largest sense. Four aspects stand out: scope, White House focus, economic coordination, and the role of Congress.

Scope

It is now necessary to include a wider variety of departments and agencies in national security policy-making and implementation than ever before. In fact, virtually every part of the executive branch has some foreign operations. Some provision must be made for their inclusion, when relevant, in the process described here. This can be achieved through flexibility in committee structures and through an NSC adviser and staff who are alert to the interests that different parts of the government have in particular issues.

White House Focus

This overlap of foreign and domestic issues strengthens the argument for centering the coordination of policy in the White House. It also demonstrates that the process cannot be limited only to the National Security Council and its offshoots. For many issues—strongly domestic in origin—it will not be possible for the council to be the primary bureaucratic focus. For many issues, the primary responsibility will fall either to the full cabinet (in exceptional cases), to institutions like the Office of Management and Budget, to the Domestic Policy Council (or its equivalent), or to some combination of them. For the sake of clarifying lines of authority, it would be useful for the president to require that the NSC adviser and the domestic policy adviser work closely together. There is also merit in having some other official, such as the White House chief of staff, act as convener. For this device to be more beneficial than harmful, however, it must be used sparingly to resolve issues that are truly crosscutting. Neither the NSC adviser nor the domestic policy adviser should have his direct access to the president impeded.

Economic Coordination

At the same time, there is an increasing need for some effective means of coordinating international economic policy, not just in and of itself, but also in relation to domestic economic issues, national security issues, and budgetary and domestic policy concerns. Indeed, this is the most complex and daunting area of policy management and the one that has, over the years, yielded least to efforts at resolving bureaucratic difficulties. For reasons given earlier, coordination must be undertaken by the White House. This activity cannot be assigned totally to any one existing body—whether in national security policy, domestic policy, or economics. Nor can it impose stifling demands on the full cabinet or lead to the appointment of a supercoordinator who would merely add another bureaucratic layer, increasing the risk of paralysis instead of reducing the chances for chaos.[18]

To a large extent, issues must be carved up and responsibilities parceled out. There should be members of each staff—such as the NSC, Domestic Policy Council, and Council of Economic Advisers—who have experience with issues affecting the other staffs. Indeed, some of these officials should act as emissaries within the government.[19]

The method of coordinating international economic policy with other matters should include such important rules of thumb as top level officials should be involved, they should be supported by a small staff, the mechanism developed should be flexible and relatively informal, it should entail a regular forum through which key economic decisions must pass, and it should be of demonstrated importance to the president.[20] Various techniques can be employed to make this process work, and responsibility for directing it should be entrusted to that official who best combines bureaucratic purview, credibility among peers, and presidential support. This probably means joint leadership by the NSC and domestic policy advisers, but trial and error in any administration will probably be needed to find a workable formula.

Most important, the next president must recognize that he needs some institutional mechanism for coordinating policy in all these areas and for presenting issues to him that can be bargained and resolved. Even more than in the traditional area of national security policy, the president needs to assert his control in this link among foreign, economic, and domestic issues.

Role of Congress

The blurring of distinctions between foreign and domestic policy—with economics cutting across both—also goes to the heart of arguments about the respective roles of the president and Congress. As made clear here, there can be no effective national security policy unless it has the backing of the American people, including the U.S. Congress. In some areas, such as the use of force, debate about the extent to which Congress can and should intervene in executive branch policy, which is as old as the Republic itself, will continue.[21] In other areas, a greater congressional role is inescapable, whatever the outcome of philosophical debate about the relative distribution of power. These areas include issues related to the economy, in which there is no clear line separating foreign and domestic policy and in which the "power of the purse strings" is also becoming increasingly important.

Congress must perforce be deeply engaged; a wise president will include the congressional factor from the initiation of policy, and congressional relations must play a central role in all international policy considerations. In this sense, it is also no longer possible to say that "partisanship stops at the water's edge," in the sense of excluding issues from domestic debate. Partisanship for its own sake can still take its toll, and creating a bipartisan basis in the traditional areas of foreign and defense policy still remains an invaluable goal. It is not possible, however, to try excluding major areas of foreign and domestic policy from the rough and tumble of congressional action. To do so is to guarantee failure. Hence, presidents should recognize the need for congressional support and take the initiative—before the inauguration or even the election.

Strategic Direction

The recommendations discussed above are designed to help make national security policy-making work with a wide variety of personnel. In effect, it is a fail-safe method, one that takes account of the way individuals tend to be selected for senior positions in the federal government, the natural competition between different parts of the bureaucracy, and the relationships that tend to develop between political appointees and career officers, both civilian and military. It is also a system designed especially to aid a president who does not have a strong background in international affairs or a strategic grasp of the United States' place in the world and the best means to advance its interests. This system should enable the president to elicit the policy views of experts with different perspectives from different parts of the government, to bring to the fore a wide variety of recommendations for dealing with particular national security issues, and to provide a means for making decisions in as informed and orderly a manner as possible.

This system of organizing for international affairs, however, cannot by itself be more than just adequate in meeting the national security challenges that will face the United States, abroad and at home, during the next several years. Indeed, this system—or any other not yet tried—will have to meet progressively higher standards as both the nature of international problems and the relevance of U.S. power change.

In brief, the United States faces a challenge to national security policy that is far more complex than at any other point since the 1940s when it became deeply involved in the outside world. At the same time, it has relatively less power to affect events—at least unilaterally—than it did in the past. This is not the result of the United States' becoming weaker. Indeed, in absolute terms, the United States is stronger than ever before, both economically and militarily. It has also regained most of the domestic political élan that was sapped by the Vietnam War and other difficulties. The shift in U.S. power is relative but, as such, it is unlikely to be fundamentally reversed.

This shift in power should not lead one to the conclusion that the United States is inevitably in decline. Along with the growth of complexity in national security, however, it does mean that U.S. leaders must be far more thoughtful and intelligent about the craft of foreign policy than at any other time in modern U.S. history.

Most important, U.S. leaders must be capable of developing and acting upon a much more strategic view of the U.S. position in the world. This strategic view must include far more attention to matching resources to demands, setting priorities, considering seemingly disparate events and actions together, making use of different instruments of policy in relationship to one another, and, to the degree possible, coordinating the activities of all parts of the government that are engaged in international affairs. In a word, the strategic view requires a rigorous, analytical, and thoughtful method of *choice*.

This process of policy-making is not alien to most other major countries. The fact that it has considerable novelty in the United States is tribute to the now-declining advantages of relative power and of the security of two broad oceans that were enjoyed during the early years of permanent U.S. engagement abroad. The lesson is simple: U.S. leaders must henceforth eschew the temptation to see the world as they would like it to be rather than how it is—the temptation to ideology. At the same time, U.S. leaders can no longer depend upon the classic U.S. penchant for viewing each foreign policy problem primarily in its own light, as though it could be met and mastered on its own and without reference to other events or to other demands upon U.S. time and resources.

There is no simple means of developing the tools that foster strategic guidance of U.S. national security policy. A prerequisite is an effective method of policy-making and policy implementation, such as the one outlined above. There must also be much more. The following are some key considerations.

Presidential Leadership

As with any other aspect of effective government, especially in an area in which the executive has such inherent powers, there can be no substitute for presidential leadership. A president need not himself have the skills and background to develop a complex strategy for U.S. national security, but he cannot avoid five tasks:
1. setting a tone for the direction he wishes the nation to take to the extent this is within both his discretion and the national tolerance for action;
2. selecting and supporting topflight, experienced officials who are able to engage in sustained strategic thinking and, through effective policy-making, are able to translate the results of this thinking into politically viable policies;
3. judging wisely among contending ideas and advocates, with an indispensable political sense that can be provided by no one other than the president;
4. exercising primary leadership in dealing with Congress, to gain support for policies or to change those that do not pass the test of comporting with basic U.S. interests, values, and aspirations; and
5. demanding that the approach outlined in these four points be central to the making and executing of U.S. policy.

Planning

Planning for international affairs must become serious business. Given the pace at which the U.S. government is often challenged to act in international affairs, it is rare that there is sustained effort to plan for future contingencies, to map out a long-term course of action, or to ground long-range policy in an abiding sense of purpose. As the Western superpower, the United States naturally often finds itself in the position of reacting to outside events. It is often difficult to mobilize domestic political support for policy change that has not been forced upon the nation by external circumstances. The failure of effective long-range planning can be traced, to a considerable degree, to defects in organization. It is usually true, for example, that to be a planner is to be irrelevant in the making and execution of current policy. Few rewards in the U.S. government go to those who become bureaucratically superfluous to the immediate work at hand.

Five important steps could help provide the U.S. government with a better chance to undertake effective, long-range planning in international affairs—although there is certainly no panacea or unfailing method for consistent success.

1. Each key cabinet member in international affairs—for example, the secretaries of state, defense, and treasury—should ensure that highly able officers serve on planning staffs; that the cabinet member actively, regularly, and visibly solicits their views; and that these individuals are rewarded in their careers. Indeed, service on a planning staff should become a sought-after—if not necessary—step in career advancement.
2. There should be a long-range planning staff as part of the NSC staff in the White House. Its personnel should be drawn largely from the relevant departments and agencies, with considerable continuity of membership from one administration to the next. From time to time, the president should meet with this national security planning staff. Indeed, there is no better bureaucratic fillip than presidential attention.
3. The NSC planning staff should work closely with institutions set up to manage crises—for example, the current Policy Review Group and its successor in the next administration—but should not share responsibilities in crisis situations, except in an advisory role.[22] This planning staff should also include personnel from, and establish effective liaison with, the White House domestic policy staff, the legislative affairs staff, and economic agencies.
4. Because of the critical need to match resources to priorities in national security, it is essential that the executive branch move purposefully toward a much more integrated international affairs budget. This budget would consider, to a degree far beyond what is practiced today, different tools of national security strategy together and provide effective means for making trade-offs. It is unconscionable that the president cannot easily make choices among, and share the political responsibility for, contending uses of funds (such as retaining a consulate abroad, expanding foreign aid or security assistance, or producing an addi-

tional military aircraft). The NSC should create a National Security Resources Board, charged with developing such a budget mechanism. The Congress must also make compromises in the way it considers budgets in these areas. Without change in both branches, the opportunity to pursue rational strategies and back them with appropriate resources will continue to elude the United States.
5. As with the overall development of a stronger capacity for strategic policy-making, the quality of top administration officials will also be key to enhancing the capacity for long-range planning.

Continuity

Incoming administrations always argue that a new president cannot impose his will on the bureaucracy unless he replaces most senior leadership with new people. No doubt there is merit in this view. Indeed, a new president brings with him a mandate to shape a basic course for the nation, and, to some extent, this is true in international as well as in domestic policy.

Yet there is always a price to be paid, at least initially, in terms of the difficulty that a new administration's team has in gaining the particular education about the outside world and about policy that can only come from government service, in learning to work together, and in developing the needed patterns of relations with the career bureaucracy. For these reasons, a lack of continuity in senior government service can at times actually impede a new administration in imposing its will on policy and certainly in exercising effective strategic leadership. To change course, there must be a thorough grounding in the facts of current policy, in relations with other countries, in tested tolerances in policy initiatives, and in the potential interactions between old and new policies and old and new government officials.

It is important, therefore, for an incoming president and his senior national security officials to strike an effective balance between retaining officials who have served the previous administration and bringing in new personnel. This is important for the morale of the career services. It is also necessary to avoid making major mistakes, especially in the early days of a new administration. Retention of knowledgeable personnel is also helpful to a new team as it seeks to gain and exercise leverage in those policy areas that are most crucial to its mandate, the new president's thinking, and the results of strategic analysis.

There is always the question about the point at which this desired continuity should begin. For the good of the nation, an administration in its latter years should recruit and advance career officers who can provide continuity because they are, at least partially, protected from partisanship. A new administration can assist in this process during the transition period by being sensitive to continuity requirements as well as to the need to impose its will and bring in individuals with party or personal loyalty to the new president. Furthermore, when recruiting new officials, there should be a premium on making use of tested individuals who have served in foreign policy posts in past administrations and who have demonstrated a capacity to work effectively within an NSC system.

Seeking continuity as a means of enhancing an administration's strategic flexibility and long-term effectiveness does argue for reducing the amount of change in senior personnel. This is the practice in West European countries, which have long faced the need to manage international affairs with relatively limited resources but more complex and difficult choices than is true, even now, of the United States. Because of U.S. political tradition, however, placing regular career officers in senior positions is never likely to happen to the extent it does in Western Europe. Indeed, as a superpower with worldwide responsibilities, the United States is significantly different from any West European state, virtually all of which face the need to adopt less flexible and more enduring foreign policy goals and methods of achieving them.

Provided that a new president places great emphasis on high-quality, seasoned appointees at all policy levels, this problem can be reduced significantly. The president can also ensure the retention of a pool of good foreign service officers by reducing the number of political appointees to ambassadorships abroad. By doing so, he can also help promote cooperation between career officers and political appointees.[23]

Bipartisanship

Continuity of process, in some form, is also a precondition for another valuable goal—the development of a greater degree of bipartisanship in U.S. national security policy than has been evident for many years. When there is strong support in the nation for a general course of action (for example, the underlying U.S. internationalism since World War II), then the task of thinking strategically is eased. Indeed, a clear strategic sense of the proper course for the nation has little value unless it can be translated into popular support.[24]

The United States has also been aided in the pursuit of greater bipartisanship in international affairs by the developments of recent years. On most key issues, differences between the two political parties have been progressively muted. On defense, strategic issues, and arms control, less separates them now than was true only half a decade ago. There is emerging bipartisan agreement about the dimensions of the economic challenge facing the United States in the world. Even in the most contentious area—the potential use of force—there has been a narrowing of differences, more now than at any other point since the early days of the Vietnam War.

As with the effort to create greater continuity in national security policy, the initiative to foster bipartisanship needs to come first from the administration in power. In each of the past several administrations, a proclamation of bipartisanship has been made once that administration has assumed office. Each administration has interpreted that goal, however, as the need for compromise by its political opponents or by Congress. To have a chance of sustenance, however, bipartisanship must develop from the opposite direction: beginning with executive branch accommodation to outside currents of thought and opinion. On arms control, for example, that has now happened. Three other potentially divisive issues on which there has been recent bipartisan success were the so-called two-track decision by the North Atlantic Council in 1979 on deployment of medium-range missiles in Europe, the recognition of U.S. vital interests in the Persian Gulf, and the decision to counter Soviet involvement in Afghanistan. In each case, policy was developed in a fashion that allowed it to gain continuity. That list now stands to be lengthened.

The objective of greater bipartisanship—as a useful underpinning for a sustainable, strategic approach to international affairs—requires efforts by the outgoing president to build bridges to his successor, as well as by the incoming president to mute the temptation for radical departures in policy, unenlightened by experience. In any event, there is a rising premium on executive branch relations with Congress—at the beginning, on a continuing basis, with majority and minority alike, and as a positive good—to build critical support for policy.

Conclusions

The arguments presented here are designed to be useful to the next president, the people he appoints, and, in particular, to those individuals in both parties who will help in the fall of 1988—or during some future change of presidents—to prepare the transition from the current administration to its successor. These transition teams should be set up as soon as possible following the national political nominating conventions. In the 73 days between election and inauguration it is practically too late for a president-elect and his advisers to begin thinking afresh about how they will govern the nation in terms of its foreign, defense, international economic, and related policies. There are events in a president's first year in office that must be planned for prior to inauguration. Nor will the new administration have the luxury after January 20, 1989 of a "honeymoon" in foreign affairs such as Congress and the American people accord a new president in domestic affairs. The world's timetable is far less geared to the U.S. electoral cycle than it was when U.S. preeminence was undisputed.

In particular, it is of great benefit to a new president to have all of his key national security appointments made and, if possible, confirmed by the Senate by inauguration day—a feat that will require congressional cooperation, as well as relaxation of some of the tedious demands made on new appointees.[25] The national security adviser and the secretaries of state and defense should be appointed as soon as possible after the election, consistent with the president-elect's certainty of choice. They will then have the capacity to direct the remaining aspects of the transition, as well as to appoint their deputies and begin the work of gaining Senate confirmation for the entire team.

It is not easy for a person who has campaigned for the presidency of the United States to adjust suddenly to actually becoming the nation's chief executive. The campaign may have consumed years. It will certainly have demanded many talents and activities that have little to do with governing—and especially not with governing in national security affairs. To the degree that this analysis helps to ease this process, it will prove its worth.

Notes

1. The term "NSC system" is used comprehensively here, encompassing the means both of making and of carrying out policy for all U.S. foreign involvements. It is viewed this way for two basic reasons: first, a legal basis for its actions in international affairs results from the National Security Act of 1947 and the sanction of the NSC; second, it is important to consider many factors in order to have a broad understanding of the nation's "security" and well-being. The terms "national security policy" and "international affairs" will thus be used more or less interchangeably.

2. The recommendations are also in large part consistent with those of the Tower Commission—the President's Special Review Board—convened to investigate the structure, organization, and operation of the NSC system after the Iran-contra affair. The commission's key conclusion was that major changes to the system are not needed, but the existing procedures should be followed. See *The Tower Commission Report* (New York: Bantam Books and *Times* Books, 1987), 87-99.

3. The director of ACDA is in the anomalous position of being both a subordinate of the secretary of state and an adviser to the NSC. This situation is the result of the act that created ACDA, however, and not the result of the National Security Act of 1947. Thus, by implication, the director's role on the council is circumscribed.

4. The next president must also decide at the outset whether the U.S. ambassador to the United Nations should be a member of either the cabinet, the National Security Council, or both. The current ambassador no longer has cabinet rank. This is a useful precedent to follow, unless the president decides that the views of a particular individual would be useful in the cabinet or the NSC.

5. An effective international affairs team must include people with three distinctly different kinds of skills: those who can chart directions for the nation, those who can devise the means for getting there, and those who have a tactical sense of what must be done immediately in any situation. Few individuals have all three skills. The capacity to integrate policy requires significant ability

in the first two skills, plus the capacity to work effectively with people who are superb tacticians.

6. A special choice facing the next president will be whether to retain the incumbent DCI. There is merit in retaining the current DCI into the next administration, if only for a transition period. It has been argued that the DCI and other Intelligence Community officials should be as objective as possible in their collection, assessment, and presentation of intelligence. This is correct; however, the DCI is in a policy-making position, even when he or she is simply conveying information. What questions are asked, how the analysis is done, and how the results are presented involve a particular perspective no mater how hard one strives for objectivity.

It is important for the DCI to be able to work effectively with other individuals in the administration and to have the background and experience to relate intelligence in perceptive ways to particular national security issues and problems. Furthermore, in relation to covert action, the DCI is perforce involved in policy-making. The next president should bear these points in mind in deciding this personnel matter.

The president also needs to decide whether to retain the President's Foreign Intelligence Advisory Board (PFIAB), which deals with the general outlines of policy, and the Intelligence Oversight Board (IOB), which was originally designed to be the president's watchdog on the Intelligence Community, particularly on covert actions. If these boards are ably led, well staffed, and have the president's confidence, both can be invaluable to him and provide another level of oversight.

In addition, an institutional mechanism for covert action decisions should be created. This has usefully been done in the regular top-level decision-making bodies of the National Security Council, centered in the White House. The president should also insist on three cardinal tests to judge the validity of covert action: it must be something that has to remain secret in order to be effective; it must produce something valuable for the United States (such as saving lives); and it must comport with U.S. values, in both means and end. Thus, the president should view the congressional committees on intelligence as valuable allies, not natural antagonists.

7. In large part, the roles and duties of other officials—such as the secretaries of state and defense—are covered by legislation. The management and organization of these departments are important, but are not the immediate concerns of the president as are the organization of the national security staff in the White House and the functioning of the overall system. The organization of the Joint Chiefs of Staff has recently been reviewed and revised; however, it is not covered here.

8. In recent years, there has been debate about whether the appointment of the NSC adviser should be subject to Senate confirmation and, thus, to requirements to testify before congressional committees later. Any president, however, will insist on having sources of strictly confidential advice. If the NSC adviser must testify, the president will seek that advice elsewhere—from someone who will, in fact, fulfill a key role of the office.

9. This function is one of the most important in the conduct of national security policy, especially when different presidential advisers have widely varying views of what should be done. Failure to agree upon what has been decided is a frequent source of confusion and error.

10. In recent administrations, these memoranda have been called, successively, National Security Study Memoranda (NSSMs), Policy Review Memoranda (PRMs), and National Security Study Directives (NSSDs). Each has served a similar set of functions in providing the president and other key officials with a formal basis for considering major policy departures. One set of documents conveying decisions taken by the president has been called National Security Decision Memoranda (NSDMs), Presidential Directives (PDs), and National Security Decision Directives (NSDDs).

11. It is conceivable that the secretary of state could act as coordinator from a White House office or even "wear two hats" by also having the position of NSC adviser. Either course would create bureaucratic controversy with other departments, however, and could deprive the president of an extra source of counsel. To facilitate the process, there would be merit in the secretaries of state, defense, and the treasury each having a small office and staff in the Old Executive Office Building, next door to the White House—the old State-War-Navy Building—as is now true of the DCI.

12. In recent administrations, the NSC adviser has had staff members who were responsible for congressional and press relations. These individuals have worked with their counterparts elsewhere in the White House, in departments, and in agencies.

13. In recent years, the size of the NSC staff—located principally in the Old Executive Office Building next to the White House—has grown considerably. No fixed number is ideal. If past practice is continued—that is, with staff officers assigned to either regional or functional areas parallel to the structure of the departments and agencies with which they principally deal—then the NSC staff needs between 25-35 senior professionals. There is also merit in having some additional, junior NSC staff members—as many as 10—primarily charged with handling the mass of routine duties that must be performed for or by the president, from presidential messages on the national days of foreign countries to legally mandated presidential submissions of tax and extradition treaties and a wealth of required reports to Congress. Historically, there has also been value in having a mixture of NSC staff people with different backgrounds (definitely including women and minorities); some from the career services and some who are brought in by a new administration from academia and elsewhere. The combination of backgrounds provides a useful means of giving the president a second look at policy alternatives.

14. In its early years, the Reagan administration attempted to manage policy through a series of Senior Interdepartmental Groups (SIGs)—primarily for foreign policy, defense, intelligence, and international economic policy. The first three had little impact, in part because they met at individual departments rather than in the White House and in part because their membership was generally below the cabinet level—that is, they could not act as effective agencies. The SIG for international economic policy did work effectively when it met in the White House Roosevelt Room—across from the Oval Office—and when its membership included top officials.

15. Thus, in the Carter administration, the NSC adviser chaired meetings of the Special Coordination Committee (SCC) on crises, arms control, and covert action—all areas that cut across major bureaucratic lines. By contrast, issues that more naturally fell within the compass of particular departments were entrusted to the chairmanship of those cabinet members. The

committee was then called the Policy Review Committee (PRC). In the Reagan administration, there has been a progressive development of committees chaired by the NSC adviser, such as the Special Arms Control Planning Group (SACPG) and the Senior Interdepartmental Group for Space. In addition, chaired by the deputy NSC adviser, there has been the Crisis Pre-Planning Group (CPPG), later renamed the Crisis Planning Group (CPG) and then the Policy Review Group (PRG). The Tower Commission recommended that all senior-level NSC committees be chaired by the NSC adviser. *The Tower Commission Report*, 96.

16. Thus, in any crisis, the State Department creates special working groups that meet around the clock to provide much of the background, information, communication, and preparatory work needed for the NSC crisis mechanism to work effectively.

17. Early in 1981, primary responsibility for managing crises was given to the vice president, through the Special Situation Group (SSG), which has met when the vice president has been in Washington and the president has not—thereby preventing a full NSC meeting from being held. This arrangement has had the advantage of having someone with a White House focus as chairman, thus avoiding problems of institutional loyalty to a department or agency. Yet such a procedure also means that the key official in managing crises is not necessarily a regular, deeply engaged member of the administration's decision-making and decision-implementing team. In crisis situations, being part of the regular conduct of national security business is essential in providing background about what is happening, the course of administrative actions, and the interactions among various key officials. This has generally been true of the last two vice presidents, but it is not always so. During the Reagan administration, over time, major responsibilities for managing crises eventually passed to the national security adviser.

18. The next president will also face the next round of debate about the locus of trade policy coordination within his administration. Various agencies—including the Office of the U.S. Trade Representative, the State Department, the Commerce Department, and the Treasury—all have legitimate claims, but no satisfactory solution has yet been found that will meet the needs of contending claimants. This area is also quintessentially about both foreign and domestic policy and about shared power between

the executive and legislative branches. The president's most important responsibility is to recognize that he must create some institutional means of coordinating and deciding trade policy and make it effective through his personal attention at key moments. The best mechanism can only be decided when other institutional arrangements involving international economic policy have been put in place.

19. For example, in the Carter administration, the official responsible for preparing the Seven Nation Economic Summits for the United States—the so-called Sherpa—reported both directly to the president and through the NSC adviser, with whom he was on excellent personal terms. He also developed relations with all economic and foreign policy departments and agencies in Washington.

20. These rules of thumb derive in large part from the effort that has come closest to succeeding: the Council on International Economic Policy. This council was created during the Ford administration and was both led and staffed from the White House.

21. Experience with the War Powers Resolution indicates that there has not been a major shift of responsibility from the executive to the Congress since the Vietnam War. The mandatory provisions of the resolution have never been invoked. Administrations have been inclined to be cautious, however, and this is probably the resolution's greatest benefit. Here, as elsewhere in national security policy, presidents should see the Congress as vital to building national support for policy or, if that support cannot be obtained, as a means of learning when to change course.

22. In a trial-and-error approach to planning, there is also great merit in developing mechanisms around specific issues—that is, task forces—to stimulate officials to see beyond immediate events or crises. Indeed, the press of concerns that have suddenly become important can be used bureaucratically to require that greater depth of analysis and foresight be applied. In these instances, however, it is important to separate personnel and meeting structure from immediate action steps, lest officials be swamped by the detail of crisis management and associated diplomacy. Thus, during the Iranian hostage crisis in 1980, a small NSC-led task force, composed of individuals not directly involved in day-to-day events, developed the policies that became the Carter Doctrine for the Persian Gulf.

23. One solution to the problem of integrating career officers and political appointees would be to place emphasis on outside individuals in making State Department appointments to levels of assistant secretary and above and to give almost all ambassadorships to members of the Foreign Service. This method would also reflect the inherent differences between diplomacy and policy-making. Diplomacy emphasizes the search for common interests with other governments, while policy-making also focuses on the use of nondiplomatic tools—including the use of force—often without reconciliation of competing interests as an objective.

24. Of course, the obverse can also be true: ideas that are patently bad for the nation can gain strong support, based on a certain stubbornness that is a hallmark of the American character. In general, however, this trait serves the nation well.

25. These demands include financial disclosure statements, divestment of some holdings, exhaustive checks into background, and the like. Some are indeed required to meet standards of ethics and security. Some go to excess. This whole set of procedures needs to be reviewed in the interest of attracting high quality individuals to government and of expediting the process, while meeting legitimate requirements concerning character and conduct.

Appendix
Checklist of Top-Priority Recommendations for Presidential Candidates and the President-Elect

Timing

- begin getting to know as many potential candidates for high office in international affairs as soon as possible in the electoral process, and pursue this effort throughout;
- appoint a transition team soon after the national nominating convention; charge it with reviewing structure, beginning to plan key events for the first year in office, and developing lists of potential candidates for senior office;
- after the election, charge the transition team to work effectively with outgoing officials and the bureaucracy, including review of existing policies and development of alternatives in high-priority areas; begin deciding on key priorities in international affairs for the first year, and complete this process before inauguration day;
- appoint cabinet-level officials and the national security adviser, as a group, within a month after the election; also decide whether to appoint a new director of central intelligence (DCI); immediately place the transition team(s) under the direction of these appointees;
- complete senior-level international affairs appointments by inauguration day, with middle level appointments to be completed soon thereafter, provided that senior officials are available to play a critical role in that process; at various levels, make some appointments from the Congress and from the opposite political party; make decisions about these presidential appointees jointly between the cabinet departments and the White House;
- express confidence in the bureaucracy; retain some incumbent officials in middle and senior-level positions, at least on an interim basis;
- decide, with top-level NSC officials, on a basic structure for the NSC system and promulgate it immediately upon inauguration; at the same time decide on the management

structure for integrating international and domestic economic policy-making with the NSC structure.

Structure

1. *National Security Council System*
- create a system of senior-level NSC interagency committees to meet in the White House (the most critical committee[s] should provide for regular meetings of top-level officials in the president's absence); provide for subordinate committees and a system of interagency working groups;
- in general, designate the NSC adviser to chair all NSC committees—at least those dealing with bureaucratically cross-cutting issues like crisis management, arms control, and covert action; if desired, however, designate appropriate cabinet members to chair NSC committees dealing with other subjects;
- create a system of policy review memoranda and presidential decision memoranda as the basis procedural tools of policy-making and promulgating key decisions; when appropriate, delegate authority for initiating policy review through this mechanism to the NSC adviser, who should work in consultation with key cabinet-level NSC members;
- create an NSC planning staff (drawing personnel primarily from the bureaucracy), provide for their career advancement, and have it meet periodically with the president; designate the NSC adviser as director of the NSC planning staff and have its meetings held in the White House;
- create a National Security Resources Board, along similar lines, to determine ways and means of integrating international affairs budgeting;
- request congressional action to make the secretary of the treasury a statutory member of the National Security Council; invite the following to take part in NSC meetings: White House chief of staff; director, Office of Management and Budget; director, Domestic Policy Council (or equivalent); director, Office of Legislative Affairs (or equivalent); chairman, Council of Economic Advisers; press secretary

and political advisers (except to the most sensitive meetings);
- other than items discussed here, make no changes to the structure of national security policy-making that require congressional action or that entail major internal reorganization, at least until after a period of settling-in and trial-and-error in the administration;
- institutionalize regular, informal weekly meetings among key NSC personnel, including the NSC adviser and the secretaries of state, defense, and treasury; follow these with informal weekly meetings between the president and key advisers, including officials such as the vice president; the NSC adviser; the secretaries of state, defense, and treasury; and the White House chief of staff;
- undertake to hold systematic presidential meetings with congressional leaders on international affairs issues in advance of crises, and broaden the scope of executive-legislative relations within each department and agency;

2. *International Economic Policy*

- create a small international economic staff in the White House to coordinate with the NSC and the Domestic Policy Council (or equivalent) and—if it is created—an Economic Policy Council; designate either the secretary of the treasury or a senior-level White House assistant to chair it; appoint a deputy to this chairman with NSC staff experience and a deputy NSC adviser with economic experience to coordinate relations between the two bodies; during the first six months, develop some workable process—according to the president's preferred style of management—for integrating trade policy with other international economic and national security policies and ensure that its mandate is understood throughout the executive branch and in Congress;

3. *Senior Appointees*

- in general, appoint officials to complement the temperament and skills of the president; ensure that the NSC

adviser, the secretaries of state, defense, and treasury, and the DCI have unimpeded access to the president, personally and in writing;
- ensure that, in every agency within the NSC system, there is at least one senior official—at first or second level—who has effective management skills and experience;
- recruit top-level officials who have the ability to think strategically and integrate conceptually the different strands of national security policy, including economics; the NSC adviser should be selected for this skill, and the secretary of state should be expected to have this ability, as well;
- within the high-level policy team, ensure a balance of national security and other international policy skills, including the abilities to develop and integrate goals, chart directions for policy, and make tactical choices;
- balance demands for diversity and variety in senior appointees with shared commitments to the president's administration and the national welfare;
- provide offices and small liaison staffs for the state, defense, and treasury secretaries in the Old Executive Office Building, to ease coordination with the NSC staff and the international economic staff;

4. *National Security Adviser*

- select an individual with broad national security experience, an ability to think conceptually and develop policy strategically, and a devotion to process and cooperation with other NSC members;
- assign the NSC adviser the tasks of ensuring information flow to the president, preparing requests for the bureaucracy on policy reviews and responses to presidential initiatives, coordinating the policy-making process (including the chairing of appropriate NSC committees), and overseeing—but not conducting—the implementation of policy;
- authorize the NSC adviser to recruit a staff of between 25-35 professionals, plus 10 junior professionals for routine business, including some holdovers from the current administration. This staff should be recruited from the ranks of the career services (military, foreign service, Intel-

ligence Community, economic agencies), academia, think tanks, business and labor, and Capitol Hill. It should ensure strong representation of women, minorities, and diverse viewpoints;
- authorize the NSC adviser to select congressional and press advisers, but make them and the NSC adviser subject to coordination and to the primary roles of the White House Office of Legislative Affairs (or equivalent) and secretary of state, respectively; authorize the NSC adviser to meet with foreign officials, but with coordination and reporting to the secretary of state as the president's chief diplomat;

5. *Cabinet Departments*

- designate the secretary of state as chief national security spokesman, after the president, although other officials (e.g., the secretary of defense and the NSC adviser) may from time to time serve as spokespersons, under the guidance of the secretary of state; assign a similar role in economics to the secretary of the treasury, but coordinated with the secretary of state and appropriate White House officials;
- reduce the percentage of non-career ambassadorial appointments; in general, favor career officers for embassies and outside appointees for international affairs positions from the level of assistant secretary and above;

6. *Intelligence*

- prior to inauguration, limit decisions on the Intelligence Community to the appointment of a new DCI, who should be from outside and have a strategic grasp of issues; consider, based on experience during the first six months, whether to separate the functions of CIA director and DCI, with the latter retaining managerial and budget authority within the Intelligence Community;
- ensure access to "competitive intelligence" from various agencies and other sources;

- appoint talented individuals, on a bipartisan basis, to the President's Foreign Intelligence Advisory Board (PFIAB) and Intelligence Oversight Board (IOB), ensure that they are effectively staffed, and use them regularly.

Leadership Choices for the 1990s

The election year creates special opportunities for policy experts to develop an agenda for the coming decade. CSIS has organized a project to marshal the best of its intellectual resources to infuse a strategic perspective into the electoral debate and to help the new administration choose foreign policy initiatives wisely.

National Security Choices for the Next President *by the CSIS Working Group on Presidential National Security Choices* cochairmen: Dennis M. Hertel, Thomas J. Ridge, and William J. Taylor, Jr.

This first monograph in the series examines five key issues: implications of arms control for conventional defense, U.S. security commitments and the implications of declining defense spending, U.S. foreign assistance, the future of the U.S. industrial base, and political limits on the use of force.

Some Guidelines on Africa for the Next President by Helen Kitchen

In the second of the 10 monograph series, Helen Kitchen addresses the following: To what extent is Africa an East-West chessboard? What is the significance for Africa and for the United States of the conspicuous Cuban presence in Africa since 1975? Which outside power has the most influence in Africa and why? What priority should we give to Africa's economic crisis? How can a more coherent Africa policy be developed?

The United States and the Asian Pacific Region: Decisions for the Next President edited by Martin E. Weinstein; contributions by Martin E. Weinstein, Eugene K. Lawson, Young C. Kim, and Frederick Z. Brown

The response to the challenges and opportunities that the United States faces in this dynamic region will, to a large extent, shape America's economic and political future, its role in the world economy, and its political leadership in the non-Communist world. This monograph examines U.S. relations with Japan, the People's Republic of China, North and South Korea, and the Philippines.

Meeting the Mavericks: Regional Challenges for the Next President by Debra van Opstal and Andrew C. Goldberg

The term "low-intensity conflict" is rapidly becoming a misnomer when applied to future conflict facing the United States in the Third World. Instead, potentially hostile states are increasingly able to strike at U.S. targets. This monograph examines the ways in which the United States can formulate an effective response.

Revitalizing U.S. Leadership in the Middle East by Robert G. Neumann, Shireen T. Hunter, and Frederick W. Axelgard

The authors examine the risks and opportunities of renewed U.S. leadership in the peace process and the costs of U.S. inaction. They look at the Soviet role and the possibility of achieving a moderate relationship with Iran, a stable Iraq, and strong pro-Western Gulf states.

Restructuring Alliance Commitments edited by Robert E. Hunter; contributions by Amos A. Jordan, Robert W. Komer, Ellen L. Frost and Harald B. Malmgren

In the last two decades, changing circumstances have dictated adjustments to U.S. relationships with alliance members. This monograph examines the U.S. commitment to NATO, Japan, and the Asian alliances and projects the needed changes and means to carry them out.

Coping with Gorbachev's Soviet Union by Stephen Sestanovich, Francis Fukuyama, Andrew C. Goldberg, Bruce D. Porter

What should the United States want in its medium to long-term relationship with the Soviet Union? This monograph examines the economic and political steps that are most conducive to achieving a strong relationship.

U.S. Global Economic Strategy: Challenges, Choices, and Priorities by John N. Yochelson

Among the topics addressed are the most effective ways of coping with the internationalization of the U.S. economy, whether the United States should promote or resist the diffusion of technology, the most effective ways of dealing with the financial debt and trade deficits, and how the United States can best cope with the consequences of its security commitments.

Organizing for National Security by Robert E. Hunter

The overall theme is procedural and institutional reform, which might enhance the efficacy of U.S. foreign and defense policy. Based on his experience at the National Security Council (NSC), the author addresses questions on the role of the NSC and interaction between the legislative and executive branches.

The Third Century: U.S.-Latin American Policy Choices for the 1990s by Georges A. Fauriol

What should the long-term strategy for the United States be in Latin America? How can this strategy be firmly grounded in a conceptually coherent and politically viable vision of opportunities and constraints?

Order Information: By phone—(202) 775-3119, by mail, or in person by visiting the CSIS Book Room. Individual books are $6.95; the entire series can be ordered for $63.00 ppd, a savings of 25 percent. **Mail to** Publications Sales Office, Center for Strategic and International Studies, 1800 K Street, N.W., #400, Washington, D.C. 20006

ALL ORDERS MUST BE PREPAID